HEALING OUT LOUD

MY RECOVERY AFTER DIVORCE

PHYLLIS WONG

Table of Contents

Acknowledgments 1

Disclaimer & Dedication 3

Introduction: 5

Chapter One: The Reluctant Yes 7

Chapter Two: Hidden Lives, Shattered Trust 9

Chapter Three: Drowning In Deception 13

Chapter Four: The Beginning Of The End 17

Chapter Five: The Breaking Point 21

Chapter Six: The Villain In His Story 23

Chapter Seven: When The Truth Comes To Light 27

Chapter Eight: When Healing Begins 31

Chapter Nine: Breaking The Cycle Of Self-Neglect 35

Chapter Ten: The Strength To Forgive 39

Chapter Eleven: Setting Boundaries For Peace 43

Chapter Twelve: The Journey To Self-Love 45

Conclusion 49

Prayer 51

Decrees 55

Notes 61

Contact And Connect 63

Copyright ©Phyllis Wong

Published by
Cole & Company Publishing House
6720 East Fowler Avenue,
Ste 161, Tampa, FL. 33617
www.colepublishinghouse.com

All rights reserved.
No part of this book may be reproduced or transmitted in any form or by any means without written permission from the publisher.

All scriptures are translated into the New King James
Version unless otherwise noted.

Scripture quotations identified as NKJV are from the New
New King James Version (NKJV). Copyright 1982 by
Thomas Nelson (Permission to use of Bible Gateway App)

Acknowledgments

First, I honor God, my Abba Father, the first and head of my life. I also honor my mother, Angela Wong-McKinnes, my family, and my church family, Life Impact Church International. Thank you for your continuous love and support.

To my children, Amani, for being the best cheerleader a mother could ask for, and Jayson, for being the greatest gift anyone could receive — I love you both more than words can express.

I want to express my heartfelt gratitude to my accountability partners — Thurman and Cassandra Thornton, Matthew and Samatha Harris, Yolanda Fabian, Chynna Ridley, Tearnee Hairston, Terri Threadcraft, Jorad Holmes, Betty Holmes, and Samantha White. Thank you for holding me accountable, for your genuine love, prayers, and unwavering support. Your acts of kindness have not gone unnoticed, and I am truly grateful.

To Brandon Lee, thank you for always showing up, being a listening ear, and for those funny TikTok videos that brought me laughter when I needed it most. Your support means more to me than you know, and I sincerely thank you.

To Unapologetically Gifted, thank you for lifting me up when I wanted to fall and keeping me busy with purpose. Thank you for standing by me when others walked away. Your Florida sister-friend loves you all deeply.

To all my saints and friends, thank you for sticking with me through it all. I see you, appreciate you, and thank you from the bottom of my heart.

Disclaimer & Dedication

Healing Out Loud is not a "bash" book! The transparency in this book isn't intended to "expose" or defame anyone. Instead, it's meant to illustrate that you can be fully committed to God while still facing challenges. I am writing and publishing this book as part of my healing journey toward wholeness. It serves as a continual reminder of God's faithfulness in my deliverance, healing, and restoration of everything the enemy thought he took from me. All of it was necessary. Without this part of my story, I might not have discovered my worth, understood the power of forgiveness, or operated in the next level of faith I needed for God to take me to my next. This is my story and how I persevered through it all and came out victorious.

This book is dedicated to anyone who has experienced divorce and needs a boost of encouragement. You are not alone, and you will get through this, even if it feels overwhelming right now. Someone else in the world is facing similar struggles, but the key difference is the grace and goodness of God. Remember, God loves you, and so do I.

Introduction:

"Moving towards progress requires us to speak the truth."
Madam Vice President Kamala Harris, The View 2024.

Divorce, or the dissolution of marriage, is a decree by a court that a valid marriage no longer exists. (Association, 2020)

According to the Centers for Disease Control and Prevention, 42% of Americans file for divorce, which averages about 86 divorces per hour. Divorce has long been stigmatized, often treated like a plague. For generations, many have endured damaging and unhealthy marriages, choosing to stay rather than face the ˑgers, trauma, and backlash associated with ˑe. In my community, especially within the divorce is a taboo subject. We are taught ˑ is "unlawful" in the eyes of God and ˑ someone who has been divorced ˑultery." As a divorcee, you may ˑssment to the body of Christ, ˑver a marriage that didn't ˑu have done nothing wrong, you can feel like you're at fault. In such times, the only place where you might find understanding is a therapist's office.

Here's the truth: no one enters marriage expecting to face The Four A's—adultery, abuse, abandonment, or addiction. Nobody wakes up and decides they want a divorce or suddenly falls out of love with their spouse. No one desires to remain in a relationship where they feel unhappy, unhealthy, unprotected, or unappreciated. People don't marry to be alone.

I certainly didn't.

Chapter One:
The Reluctant Yes

I first met my ex-husband in 2013 while I was serving as a worship leader at a local church. He was a member of the congregation. We were drawn to each other, but at the time, I had just made the difficult decision to give my son up for adoption, and I wasn't in a place to start a new relationship.

Nearly a decade later, in 2022, I was part of another church community when he reappeared in my life. Although he began showing interest in me, I was hesitant and avoided his advances. I was still healing from a recent heartbreak that had left me feeling bitter and broken, making me unprepared for any serious commitment. Whenever he referred to me as his wife, my response was always the same: "Not me."

Whenever the church's leadership team would tell me, "He's going to be your husband," my response was always, "No, he's not." I decided to be completely upfront one evening at the Elder's house, hoping it would scare him away. I introduced myself plainly, "Hi, my name is Phyllis Wong. I have two kids out of wedlock. Although I don't kiss and tell, the rumors about me being promiscuous are mostly true—eight out of ten, to be exact. I can give you names and numbers because I have nothing to hide and nothing to lose. I know I'm a lot to handle, so if you think you can manage, be my guest. But if I'm too much, now is the time to say so because one thing I won't do is waste your time or mine. Any questions?"

Instead of running away, he simply said, "OK," as if what I had just revealed was no big deal. I expected our courtship to be long and thoughtful, but every other conversation turned into, "Let's get married. I don't want to wait." I began to feel backed into a corner, pressured into marriage by the ministry's growing focus on having a married leadership team. It felt as if being single was undesirable, and I eventually gave in. We exchanged rings and vows on April 8th, 2022, and were married at the Elder's kitchen table.

Chapter Two:
Hidden Lives, Shattered Trust

From the beginning, I was open and honest, addressing the rumors surrounding me, answering his questions, and doing my best to ease his insecurities. However, as time passed, secrets he had kept hidden from me began to surface, and he struggled to deal with my reactions.

One time, a woman knocked on our door, asking for her house key back. He stormed out, ready to confront her, and I had to physically restrain him, pinning him against the truck to calm him down. As I approached the woman, she quickly drove off but called him moments later, asking, "Baby, are you okay?" When asked if I was okay, he was taken aback by how calm I was.

There were other times when I confronted him about his conversations with other women, where he'd say he was going to divorce me and that he never really loved me. I was hurt, emotional, and feeling lost.

On another occasion, we arrived at church, but he stayed in the truck the entire time. When I went to check on him, he exploded, saying he wanted a divorce and couldn't be the man he wanted to be because he felt smothered. Instead of reacting angrily, I simply walked away, determined not to let him see me cry. As I walked, I could hear him arguing with the Elder down the road, but I kept moving forward. When he finally caught up to me, I kissed him and told him that I would wait for him because I didn't get married to get a divorce. Once again, he was shocked because my reaction wasn't what he expected.

The lies he told me at the beginning of our relationship started to unravel. He had told me that his mother, stepfather, brother, and sister had passed away. I was devastated and felt deep empathy for him. However, after we got married, we went to his family's home to evacuate during Hurricane Ian, and I was shocked to discover that the mother and stepfather, whom I believed had died, were very much alive—and eager to meet me. They had heard wonderful things about me, but I was completely unaware that they were still living.

When I confronted him about this, he explained, "I wanted to protect my family from women who might want to hurt me." As I got to know them, I also found out that his brother and sister were alive, and, to my surprise, our parents and my uncle had all gone to high school together. I knew this revelation made him uncomfortable, and after that encounter, I never saw his family again.

Chapter Three: Drowning in Deception

I exhausted every effort to save my marriage, even when it drained me emotionally, mentally, physically, and spiritually. I was willing to remain in a situation that I knew was unhealthy because the thought of being alone was too much to bear. I followed every piece of advice and every suggestion, but nothing seemed to work.

What do you do when everything you try only makes things worse? What do you do when you apply biblical principles to your marriage, hoping for restoration, but instead, it keeps spiraling downward? What do you do when you fulfill the role of a godly wife, yet your husband disappears for days? What do you do when your husband chooses to sleep in his car because the living conditions he created are too unbearable? What do you do when you find yourself fighting for your marriage alone?

I spent the last four months of my marriage feeling completely alone, and despite my efforts to hide it, the depression became increasingly apparent. From October to January, I fought desperately against the inevitable, believing and praying that somehow the lies he had told would become truth, that I could prove everyone wrong, including myself. But instead, each lie hit me like a massive tsunami, overwhelming me and making it nearly impossible to fight or forgive. The harder I tried to hold on, the more I felt myself drowning.

The disconnect between us was undeniable, and whenever I tried to get him to see that something was wrong or when I voiced my concerns, he would ignore me, make me feel like I was crazy, and dismiss my feelings as inadequate.

When I began receiving messages and photos of him with another woman in bed, I would show him everything—the Facebook messages, the emails, and my responses—only to have my feelings brushed aside. He insisted that these women were "lying," that these were "past relationships," and that I shouldn't "dwell on them."

Whenever I asked where he'd been after disappearing for two or three days, he would tell me he'd been staying at his aunt's house. I would suggest he go "wash himself," and he would get angry. He always smelled too clean for someone who supposedly worked in a hospital, a nursing home, a bread factory, and a cement factory.

When I shared these feelings with my counselors, they all gave me the same advice — pray. Pray and ask the Lord to help you communicate with your husband effectively. Pray and ask the Lord to restore the bridge in your marriage. But I was tired of praying and seeing no results. I was tired of giving my husband a pass for things I wouldn't tolerate from a stranger on the street. I was tired of throwing away home-cooked meals because he didn't come home. I was tired of fixing things I didn't break. I was tired of living paycheck to paycheck, barely scraping by, because my husband, who claimed to be working 40+ hours, wasn't bringing home a check. I was tired of the dishonesty and deception. I was tired of the phone calls and texts filled with incriminating evidence. I was tired of defending our name and fighting for this marriage all by myself.

I was tired of begging my husband to be my husband.

Contrary to popular belief, I supported my husband in every venture he pursued. I endorsed and promoted his "Ministry of Movement" and his "construction business." Despite what he may have thought, I defended him in more ways than one. I often found myself standing up for him, becoming a co-conspirator by repeating the lies he told. Whenever he pulled a "no call, no show," I would cover for him. I painted a picture of him as a wonderful husband to save face, even though I didn't believe the words coming out of my mouth.

Chapter Four:
The Beginning of the End

November 2022 marked the beginning of the end. One Saturday evening, while I was ministering in Plant City, Florida, I began to experience an excruciating pain unlike anything I had ever felt before. I couldn't stand, sit, or lie down without immense discomfort. The following day, after much persuasion, we went to the hospital. What I initially thought was just a bad case of gas turned out to be something much more severe, and I had to be admitted.

At first, the doctors suspected it was an issue with my kidneys. Still, after a week in the hospital, they diagnosed me with choledocholithiasis—gallstones in my bile duct—and discovered I had over 200 gallstones in my gallbladder. Emergency surgery was necessary. The day before my scheduled surgery, he told me he would be back, but he never returned. After my surgery, he didn't answer any of my calls to check on me. It wasn't until my mother told me that he had packed his things and left that I realized he was gone. His reason? He said he left to "finish a house project in Dade City" because he "couldn't bear to see me in the hospital broken." I knew it wasn't true, yet I still tried to support him.

I spent two weeks and a day in the hospital, including Thanksgiving Day, which I spent alone watching NFL football games. I had never felt so isolated, and the depression became overwhelming.

My spirit was heavy as I began to mourn the death of my marriage. I mourned the husband I never truly had, the broken covenant and the lost dreams. The weight of it all was so overwhelming that I felt I might lose my mind if it hadn't been for a woman named Cynthia Bell, an eighty-year-old Jamaican woman who worshipped God from the bed next to mine. She reminded me that God can do anything but fail.

When I wanted to stay in bed, she would call the nurse and insist that I walk the hallways, urging me to do so if I wanted to go home. When I had no appetite, she made sure I ate so I could have a bowel movement. It was hard to say no to her, as she reminded me so much of my Grandma Phyllis. Her worship was so contagious that I couldn't help but join in.

When I was released from the hospital, I waited with anticipation to see him. But when I got home, I was informed that he was "going from Dade City to Gainesville to complete his doctorate while working as an intern at the local children's hospital." No matter how much I tried to put a positive spin on it or make excuses, deep down, I knew he was running away.

I was done pleading with him to stay where he no longer wanted to be. I was done begging him to be the husband he once claimed he wanted to be. I couldn't find the strength to convince him to stay any longer. The last time I saw him, I had packed up the rest of his things, ready for him to take. As I said my goodbyes, I knew in my heart that he wasn't coming back.

Chapter Five: The Breaking Point

Throughout his time in Gainesville, our conversations over the phone were brief, rarely lasting more than five minutes. One night, while my ex-husband was supposedly at "work" and "too busy to call," I broke down and wept. At that moment, I surrendered completely to God, saying, "If this is your will, I will endure until the end; but if it isn't, you're going to have to remove him from my life because I no longer have the strength to keep fighting, and I'm tired of pretending everything is fine. Whatever you decide, I will be content."

I had reached the end of my rope. I was done with the emotional and verbal abuse, the gaslighting, and the anxiety that had taken root in my life—something I had never experienced before. I finally accepted the reality that my marriage was over. I was done.

February 2023 was when everything finally came to a head. The last straw was when he lied about getting me a car, and I was still left begging for rides to my engagements. I'd had enough. I blocked him from calling or reaching out to me after being privately disrespected and publicly humiliated for the last time.

During this period, we were instructed not to contact each other, to give ourselves time to cool down, and to communicate when we were both calm. Instead, he sent me videos about being a submissive wife and how a godly wife should behave. He even threatened that if I didn't get my act together, he would file for divorce. But I beat him to it. I went to the courthouse and filed the paperwork myself. I've never been the type to write checks that couldn't be cashed.

Chapter Six:
The Villain in His Story

After filing and processing the paperwork, I sent him an email, making sure to cc my spiritual leaders. I wanted everything to be clear and on record, ensuring nothing I said could be taken out of context. The abuse that I had chosen to overlook for so long had finally become undeniable and crucial to address. Despite his attempts to persuade me not to go through with the divorce, the peace and reassurance I felt in my spirit far outweighed his objections. I knew deep down that this was the right decision.

I wanted to meet with him for a "closure conversation," but that meeting never occurred. He became angry when he realized the meeting wasn't about us getting back together and refused to engage.

His last email included a part that read, "You have never shown courtesy toward me or my feelings. All you've done is undermine them. In every relationship you've been in, you've played the victim. When are you going to stop acting like 'woe is me' and be real? You will not corrupt my spirit like you and your family have done throughout this...whatever you call this. It's crazy how you can go to Auntie's church and 'prophesy,' knowing full well that you don't even believe what you sing or say. You are so broken and beaten down by Satan that you can't even see that your sacrifice is soiled and spoiled. Our gifts are given to us without repentance, so you can continue to operate in yours, soiled and defeated as you've always been. You can keep your last name Wong because my family aren't pushovers or quitters."

I laughed and replied, "OK," knowing that no matter what I said, he wouldn't listen to reason. The people who knew his side of the story quickly became the prosecutor, the judge, and the jury, labeling me as "a liar," "a quitter," and "a hypocrite." Someone even said I was out of order for filing for divorce, claiming I was making God a liar. Another person suggested I give him an alternative instead of calling it quits. Although I wanted to defend my reasons, character, integrity, and name, I chose not to. Instead, I held onto the scripture, "The LORD will fight for you; you need only to be still" (Exodus 14:14, NKJV). This verse helped me remain unbothered by his actions, resist reacting to subliminal messages, and ignore the opinions of people whose views once mattered but no longer held weight.

Let me be clear: I loved my husband. I loved him when I didn't want to. I loved him even when he wasn't my choice. I loved him despite feeling pressured. I loved him when disrespect showed up at my front door. I loved him beyond the red flags, past my disappointments, and through the bad he saw in himself. I loved him through every lie, every scandal. I loved him through it all. There was nothing anyone could tell me about him that I didn't already know, or so I thought.

After everything was said and done, I didn't mind being seen as the villain in this marriage. I'm willing to be wrong; I'll acknowledge and accept that the downfall of this marriage was my fault. I'll take the blame for not holding it down as I should have, walking away when things got hard, and not being the Proverbs 31 wife. I'll admit I didn't stand up and defend my husband against my family. I didn't mind being seen as the jerk.

Chapter Seven:
When the Truth Comes to Light

During one of our arguments, I said, "Most women wouldn't let you get away with what I've been overlooking. One of these days, you'll stop abusing the grace I've shown you. You'll get caught up, and when that happens, I won't be there to cover for you or bail you out." He dismissed my words, not taking them seriously. Sometimes, you have to let people face the consequences of their actions. I firmly believe that when God chooses to expose us, it's not humiliating us but saving us from ourselves. And that's exactly what happened in April 2023.

I was on my way home from an engagement when I received a phone call. The question I was asked left me shocked and embarrassed: "Did you know that your husband was in jail over a month ago, and he's been calling us, asking for money?" Jail? Asking for money? MY HUSBAND? No way! I responded honestly, and after we hung up, I felt numb. What could he have done to get himself locked up in Alachua County?

The day after the phone call, I was invited to lunch. During lunch, I was presented with the answer I had been dreading. Staring at his mugshot and reading the police report confirmed everything I had felt in my spirit. He had been arrested for domestic violence, resisted arrest by violently kicking the police cruiser, nearly injuring a nearby officer, and had to be Baker Acted. He was released a month later because the victim didn't appear in court.

The betrayal wasn't just a personal wound—it was public record. The offense had occurred precisely three months to the day after my surgery, and the incident stemmed from a "recurring conversation about his past marriage." The more I stared at the report, the angrier I became. He wanted to play checkers while I played chess. He made his move, and when my move ended the game, he played the victim.

I excused myself, went to the ladies' room, and wept. I wasn't crying because I was sad—I was crying because, once again, I had been humiliated.

It's often said that "love covers over a multitude of sins," but I was devastated to realize that my love for him wasn't enough. I felt humiliated because I had warned him, yet he still managed to make both of us look bad, especially since, by law, I was still his wife. However, this situation also left me with a sense of gratitude and validation. It confirmed that God does speak to me and that the feelings I had since October were accurate and true.

I was grateful that he left before the abuse turned physical. I silently thanked God because, for the first time, I could breathe without my chest hurting. I was no longer consumed by stress over this situation. The storm he left me in was finally starting to pass, and after months of darkness, I could finally see the sunshine and rainbows.

Chapter Eight: When Healing Begins

Healing is becoming free from pain and becoming sound or healthy again.

Healing was something I never thought I could achieve, nor did I feel I deserved it. This marriage had taken so much from me, and I had refused to allow myself to feel the pain fully. I didn't want to admit that I had failed. I didn't want to acknowledge that my best wasn't enough. I couldn't afford to break and didn't want to be seen as weak. Yet, God never saw me as weak. God saw what I viewed as a punishment for my past as an invitation to draw closer to Him.

I was so disappointed in myself and my decisions that I didn't want to speak to anyone, not even the Lord. It wasn't until I stopped hiding from my hurt and confronted the good, the bad, and the indifferent that my healing truly began.

"He heals the brokenhearted and binds up their wounds." —Psalm 147:3. "'But I will restore you to health and heal your wounds,' declares the Lord." — Jeremiah 30:17

In my healing process, I had to confess some things out loud to break the cycle. I had to admit that I have a habit of making people who exhibit bad behavior look good at my own expense. I had to confess that I often accepted anything and everything in the name of love. I took ownership of the fact that I chose to stay even when he repeatedly showed me his true character. I had to confess that accepting less than what I truly deserved was easier. I had to confront the painful truth of my experience and hear it out loud. I could no longer soothe myself with lies.

One major problem in our marriage was our terrible communication. While I understood his defensiveness, he misunderstood my posture and silence. For the longest time, I struggled with the sound of my voice. Now, I know what you might be thinking—how could a radical worshipper, Florida's Princess of Praise,

When Healing Begins

someone whose praise is so loud and contagious, struggle with her voice? But the truth is, I always struggled with being heard. I felt like no one ever really listened to my feelings or what I had to say, so I went mute, especially in my marriage. Whenever I was asked for my opinion, it was never received or respected, but when someone else said the same thing I did, it was suddenly "received" and "of God."

What do you do when the voice that heals the nations can't cure the pain in your home? What do you do when your voice is powerful to others, but you're forced into silence in the name of "submission"? What do you do when competing with your spouse instead of completing him? What do you do when you've hit rock bottom?

I asked myself these questions, and the answer was so simple. It was only when I reached the lowest point in my life that I became open to welcoming the greatest change.

Chapter Nine:
Breaking the Cycle of Self-Neglect

I had to learn to be selfish. For years, I had been selfless, always busy being there for everyone else and showing up for others, but I didn't know how to show up for myself. I had to start showing up in ways that made me uncomfortable. I had to apologize to myself— many times. I apologized for expecting others to act like I would. I apologized for treating myself as less important than others. I apologized for not setting and maintaining my boundaries. I apologized for not letting people go when they first started showing signs of being untrustworthy. I apologized for disrespecting myself and allowing others to do the same.

At the same time, I had to stop apologizing for things that weren't my fault. I had to remind myself that the things my ex-husband did were not a reflection of me. It took a long time to believe I hadn't done anything wrong. Even though he was gone, the gaslighting had taken such a toll on me that I took responsibility for his behavior. There was a time when survivor's guilt was at its peak. I went to everyone my ex-husband had befriended and apologized. I felt like I had to clean up everything I thought he had messed up. Although most were forgiving, one person said, "Phyllis, although I appreciate your apology, you're not the person I want to hear from. You no longer have to apologize for his life decisions. You honored your vows, and you did nothing wrong."

When I realized I could either hold on to the shame of his actions or let it go, I chose to let the shame go. I decided that I would no longer be the victim. Over time, I felt a freedom I never knew existed.

I had to stop expecting people who drained me to replenish me. I had to stop calling everyone for advice. Instead, I turned inward, fasted, and prayed for myself. I asked God to show me who Phyllis really was—show me the things in me that weren't pleasing to Him, the things I could change instead of focusing on what I couldn't. I began to point the finger at myself, asking the hard questions and making Phyllis a priority.

I came to understand that self-care isn't an expense or a burden but a necessity. Taking myself out to eat and going to the movies alone became the norm. I began to invest in myself so that I could no longer use the excuse, "I didn't have the means to do it." Putting myself first allowed me to experience myself in a new and fulfilling way.

Chapter Ten:
The Strength to Forgive

"When a deep injury is done to us, we never heal until we forgive." - *Nelson Mandela.*

One of the hardest things I had to do was practice forgiveness daily. In the first few months, as my divorce was being finalized, forgiveness felt like a curse word to me. It was something I didn't want to do. I fought hard against it because I desired vengeance; I wanted him to feel just a fraction of the pain he had caused me. I wanted him to suffer. Yet, even in those moments, I pushed myself to forgive—not because it was easy, but because I knew that holding on to bitterness would only drain my energy and keep me connected to the very thing I was trying to break free from. I had to forgive all parties involved, even when I knew they weren't sorry. I had to learn to move on—with love—because I realized that life doesn't wait for you to get yourself together.

People often ask me, "How did you manage to do that?" My response was simple: Whenever I thought of an offense or recalled a hurtful conversation, I would say, "I forgive that." I would repeat, "I forgive..." until the memory no longer stung, until it no longer had power over my emotions. Forgiveness doesn't excuse the other party; it frees you from the past and enlarges your future and your territory.

One day, I was checking my Facebook messages and noticed he had messaged me. I didn't respond until the day after our divorce was finalized. Whether he forgave me or not didn't matter because I wasn't forgiving him for his sake—I was forgiving him for mine.

After sending him the divorce documents, I attached a message that read:

"Attached to this message is the legal proof you requested in February 2023. As of today, the divorce has been finalized. I want to take this moment to apologize to you. I apologize for not being whole enough to be your companion. I apologize for not having enough faith to believe in restoring this marriage. I apologize for pushing down my feelings in the name of peace and silencing my voice in the name of submission, which made you think I didn't defend you or us. I apologize for making you my idol instead of my helpmate, for putting you in a place where only God belongs and expecting you to bear the weight of it. I apologize for making you feel like I listened to others and not to you. I apologize for every hurt I caused you. I apologize for moving too quickly with you. I apologize for not listening the first time when you said, 'I want a divorce,' in the church parking lot after you got caught cheating the second time. I apologize for not being the wife you prayed for. I recognize and acknowledge my faults, flaws, and the part I played in destroying this marriage.

This is my prayer for you: God continues to enlarge your territory. I pray that God opens the doors and windows of heaven and gives you the desires of your heart. I pray that you are made whole from the crown of your head to the soles of your feet. I pray that you are fully healed in every area of your life. I pray that God continues to shower down favor upon you. I pray you've learned the lessons you needed to learn so you won't have to repeat this season. I pray that you know you are forgiven, that, above all else, you are still God's son.

I pray that we never be friends, that we never reconcile our differences, that you manifest where you are, and that we never have to speak again because reconciliation is not an option. Sometimes, God tears things apart—deliberately and completely—so that they can be rebuilt and restructured, and I pray that God rebuilds you from the ground up. Amani and I forgive you. We release you. We pray and wish you well in all things in Jesus' name."

Getting to a place of forgiveness is not an easy journey. It's not for the immature or the weak. You'll know you're on the right path when you start to feel your power returning and begin to experience true freedom.

Chapter Eleven:
Setting Boundaries for Peace

"And the peace of God, which passeth all understanding, shall keep your heart and minds through Christ Jesus."
Philippians 4:7

I permitted myself to go through the stages of grief—denial, anger, bargaining, depression, and accept-ance. I allowed myself to feel the pain, to let it hurt, but I didn't allow the pain to take up permanent residence in my heart. I didn't let grief cloud my judgment or throw a pity party. I refused to let grief disrupt my peace. It's true what they say: once you emerge from a storm, you won't look like what you've been through. There were days when I didn't know how to survive because this storm should have taken me out. There were days when simply getting through was a blessing.

In the letter to my ex-husband, I said, "I pray that we never be friends. I pray that we never reconcile our differences. I pray that you manifest where you are and never have to speak to me again because reconciliation is not an option." I meant every word. Some might say this makes me sound bitter, but I assure you, I'm not. I am setting boundaries for future encounters because I know our paths will cross again, especially in the industry I'm in. The difference this time is that I can say, "Hey, God bless you," and keep it moving—because my peace requires that. I won't allow the memories of what was done to me to disrupt my peace, including his presence. I value my peace more than saving face. This has given me the freedom and permission to live and rest in peace.

Chapter Twelve:
The Journey to Self-Love

"Be the love you never received." - Rune Lazuli.

The hardest lesson I had to learn was how to love myself again. I couldn't let the hurt caused by someone else stop me from receiving the love I deserved. I couldn't make others pay for mistakes they didn't make. I recently talked with my brother about this, and he didn't like what I had to say. I told him, "I'm not thinking about my love life or being someone's special lady right now. I'm completely unlovable. I feel love has forgotten me, like it will never find me. I'm at a place where if love never finds me, I will be okay if I never get to experience the physical melody of my heart's song." The more I thought about it, the more disappointed in myself I became. How could I allow myself to feel this way? This isn't who I am — I love love.

I love the idea of love, that genuine agape love, the kind so pure it would make the average person sick. The type of love that doesn't need to be hidden behind closed doors, the kind that declares to the heavens that you are THE ONE, not just an option. The type of love that doesn't need the approval of onlookers, the kind that's worth fighting for that can stand the test of distance and time, inspiring generations to come. That unexplainable yet understandable love—the kind that laughs at the simplest things and enjoys the moment's love offers—the love that takes hard work and dedication, the love that 1 Corinthians 13 exemplifies. Realistically, I know I'll never experience that love until I heal and can experience that love for myself—by myself.

I always second-guess a good thing. I always question whether I'm good enough or worthy enough to receive such a gift. For a long time, I didn't think I was worthy; I pushed people away, tormented by my past, which haunted my vision and clouded my judgment. I ran away from what could be, but I knew that if I wanted to get this right, I needed to figure it out for my betterment to set the foundation appropriately. Instead of walking away, I sat down and did the work. I looked at myself in the mirror and declared small affirmations daily:

I am beautiful, inside and out, for I was "created in the image of God" (Genesis 1:27).

I am powerful beyond measure and chosen, for I am a "chosen generation, a royal priesthood..." (1 Peter 2:9).

I am courageous and bold, for I am "fearfully and wonderfully made" (Psalm 139:14).

I am successfully unstoppable, for I can do "all things through Christ" (Philippians 4:13).

And most importantly, I am loved by God, for God has loved me "with an everlasting love" (Jeremiah 31:3).

I've come to realize that when you speak life and encourage yourself, love will eventually come. I'm at a point where, no matter what happens to me, I will no longer give my past permission to run my life. Despite my past, I still believe in love. Despite my past, I still have love to offer someday. It may not be for me right now, but one day, I know that love will remember me and find me. And when it does, love will trust me enough to handle and love it back.

Conclusion

Everyone's journey is different, and my healing process was far from easy—it was turbulent at times. It took me a while to reach this place of freedom, but I've come to understand that this suffering had a purpose; this journey was meant to be a testimony for someone else, showing how to overcome the trauma, triggers, drama, and backlash of divorce. Acknowledging that things will never be the same is part of reclaiming every negative experience you've encountered on this journey.

To the person reading this, I want to encourage you. Healing is your portion. Healing is what you deserve. You deserve to wake up without the weight of this season pressing on your chest. You deserve to walk by your favorite places without being triggered. No, you didn't sign up for disappointment, disrespect, or humiliation—but don't give up on God, for He will never leave you nor forsake you, and don't give up on yourself. You are stronger than you think. You survived what millions couldn't. Healing and wholeness won't happen overnight, but I guarantee you'll become the best version of yourself as you make it through this. You may not see it right now, but you will make it through. How do I know that? Because if God did it for me, I know He can do it for you too.

I challenge you to live. Live with purpose. Live for purpose.

Get up and LIVE...

... because I won't let you die here!

Prayer

Heavenly Father,

I come before You today with a heart that is heavy and burdened by the pain and trauma of divorce. The feelings of rejection and abandonment have left deep wounds in my soul, but I know that You are the God who heals and restores. Your Word says that You are close to the brokenhearted and that You save those who are crushed in spirit (Psalm 34:18, NKJV). I ask that You draw near to me now, Father, and bring healing to every part of my being.

Lord, You are the One who binds up the wounds of the brokenhearted and heals all of their hurts (Psalm 147:3). I lay my pain, my heartache, and my feelings of rejection and abandonment at Your feet. I ask that You replace these feelings with Your peace that surpasses all understanding (Philippians 4:7). Let Your love flood my heart and mind, washing away every trace of sorrow and despair.

Father, I ask for Your restoration in every area of my life that has been affected by this divorce. Your Word declares that You will restore the years that the locust has eaten (Joel 2:25). I claim that promise over my life right now. Restore my joy, peace, hope, and sense of purpose. Help me to see myself through Your eyes—as Your beloved child, cherished and valued beyond measure (1 John 3:1).

Lord, I ask for deliverance from the chains of rejection and abandonment that have held me captive. Your Word says that You have not given me a spirit of fear, but of power and of love and of a sound mind (2 Timothy 1:7). I declare that I am no longer a prisoner to these negative emotions. I am free in Christ, and whom the Son sets free is free indeed (John 8:36).

Father, help me forgive myself and my ex-spouse for any wrongs that have been committed. I choose to release any bitterness, anger, or resentment, and I ask that You fill my heart with Your love and compassion (Ephesians 4:31-32). I know that unforgiveness can hinder my healing, so I ask for Your grace to forgive fully and completely.

Lord, I ask that You guide me as I move forward. Lead me in Your truth and teach me, for You are the God of my salvation; on You, I wait all the day (Psalm 25:5). Help me to trust in Your plan for my life, even when I cannot see the way forward. I believe that You are working all things together for my good, according to Your purpose (Romans 8:28)

Thank You, Lord, for being my refuge and strength, a very present help in trouble (Psalm 46:1). I trust You to carry me through this season and to bring me out on the other side, stronger and more resilient than before. I praise You for the healing, restoration, and deliverance that is taking place in my life, and I give You all the glory.

In the mighty name of Jesus, I pray. Amen.

Decrees

These decrees are powerful declarations that align your heart and mind with God's truth, His Word. When you make a decree, God establishes it, and it becomes a law in the earth.

1. I decree that I am healed from the pain of divorce, and God is restoring my soul (Psalm 23:3).
2. I decree that I am walking in God's peace, which surpasses all understanding, guarding my heart and mind (Philippians 4:7).
3. I decree that my past no longer defines me but by God's purpose for my life (Jeremiah 29:11).
4. I decree that every broken place in my life is healed and made whole by God's love (Psalm 147:3).
5. I decree that the joy of the Lord is my strength, and I will not be shaken (Nehemiah 8:10).

6. I decree that I am free from the pain of rejection, for I am accepted in the Beloved (Ephesians 1:6).
7. I decree that I am overcoming every emotional wound with the comfort of the Holy Spirit (John 14:26).
8. I decree that I have the strength to move forward and will not be held back by my past (Philippians 3:13-14).
9. I decree that I am resilient, and God is turning my mourning into dancing (Psalm 30:11).
10. I decree that I am victorious over the trauma of divorce, and I walk in God's abundant life (John 10:10).
11. I decree that I am surrounded by God's unfailing love, which never leaves or forsakes me (Hebrews 13:5).
12. I decree that the Great Physician is mending my heart, and I am whole again (Psalm 147:3).
13. I decree that the pain of divorce will not define me but by the destiny, God has for me (Romans 8:28).

14. I decree that I walk in forgiveness, releasing any bitterness or anger that may linger (Ephesians 4:31-32).
15. I decree that God is restoring my joy and filling me with His peace (Romans 15:13).
16. I decree that I am free from the spirit of heaviness, and I put on the garment of praise (Isaiah 61:3).
17. I decree that I am strong in the Lord and in the power of His might (Ephesians 6:10).
18. I decree that God is redeeming my life from destruction and crowning me with lovingkindness and tender mercies (Psalm 103:4).
19. I decree that I am walking in the fullness of God's love, which casts out all fear (1 John 4:18).
20. I decree that God is renewing my mind, and I am being transformed by His Word (Romans 12:2).
21. I decree that I am a new creation in Christ, and the old has passed away (2 Corinthians 5:17).

22. I decree that I am filled with hope, for God is my refuge and strength (Psalm 46:1).
23. I decree that I am no longer a victim of divorce but a victor in Christ Jesus (Romans 8:37).
24. I decree that God is restoring everything the enemy has stolen, and I will recover all (Joel 2:25).
25. I decree that I am walking in freedom, for where the Spirit of the Lord is, there is liberty (2 Corinthians 3:17).
26. I decree that God loves me, and His perfect love is healing every broken place in my heart (Psalm 34:18).
27. I decree that I am valuable in God's eyes and fearfully and wonderfully made (Psalm 139:14).
28. I decree that I am strong and courageous, for the Lord my God is with me wherever I go (Joshua 1:9).
29. I decree that I am resilient, and God is giving me beauty for ashes, the oil of joy for mourning, the garment of praise for the spirit of heaviness; (Isaiah 61:3

30. I decree that I am walking in God's purpose and destiny for my life, and I will fulfill the plans He has for me (Jeremiah 29:11

Notes

Association, A. B. (2020, December 03). American Bar Association. Retrieved from www.americanbar.org: https://www.americanbar.org/groups/legal_services/milvets/aba_home_front/information_center/family_law/marriage_and_divorce/annulment_separation_divorce/ending_the_marriage/divorce/

Contact And Connect

Social Media:

www.facebook.com/iamPhyllisWong

www.instagram.com/iamPhyllisWong

www.tiktok.com/iamPhyllisWong

Email:

bookphylliswong@gmail.com

Website:

https://iamphylliswong.weebly.com